DC vs Marvel
The Rise of Superheroes and Their Epic Battle

Noah Shaw

Copyright © 2024 by Noah Shaw

All rights reserved. No part of this book may be reproduced, distributed, or transmitted in any form or by any means, including photocopying, recording, or other electronic or mechanical methods, without the prior written permission of the author, except in the case of brief quotations embodied in critical reviews and certain other noncommercial uses permitted by copyright law.

This book was created with the assistance of artificial intelligence tools, which were used to research, organize, and develop the content. Final edits and creative direction were overseen by the author.

Disclaimer:

The characters, stories, and trademarks mentioned in this book are the properties of their respective owners, including DC Comics and Marvel Comics. This book is an independent work of analysis and commentary, created under fair use principles. It is not affiliated with or endorsed by DC Comics, Marvel Comics, or any of their subsidiaries.

Table of Content

INTRODUCTION: A TALE OF TWO UNIVERSES 5

CHAPTER 1: ORIGINS AND EVOLUTION 8

CHAPTER 2: THEMATIC DIFFERENCES 12

CHAPTER 3: ICONIC CHARACTERS SHOWDOWN 18

CHAPTER 4: THE CINEMATIC RIVALRY 23

CHAPTER 5: FAN CULTURES 27

CHAPTER 6: COLLABORATION AND CROSSOVERS 31

CHAPTER 7: THE BUSINESS SIDE 34

CHAPTER 8: THE EVOLUTION OF ART AND DESIGN 38

CHAPTER 9: VIDEO GAMES AND INTERACTIVE MEDIA .. 45

CHAPTER 10: THE BUSINESS OF LICENSING AND MERCHANDISE 52

CHAPTER 11: THE RISE OF STREAMING AND DIGITAL MEDIA 60

CONCLUSION: A LEGACY OF HEROES 66

REFERENCES 69

Introduction: A Tale of Two Universes

The Birth of a Phenomenon

Imagine a world without superheroes—no caped crusaders patrolling the night, no web-slinging vigilantes soaring between skyscrapers, no epic battles for the fate of humanity. It's a world nearly impossible to conceive, as superheroes have become more than fictional characters; they are cultural icons, modern myths that inspire, entertain, and define generations. At the heart of this phenomenon lies a rivalry that has spanned nearly a century: DC and Marvel.

DC Comics introduced the world to superheroes as we know them today, with Superman's debut in ACTION COMICS #1 in 1938. Larger than life and rooted in mythic archetypes, DC's heroes inspired awe and wonder. Marvel, arriving later, carved its niche by creating characters who were flawed, relatable, and grounded in everyday struggles. Together, these two titans revolutionized storytelling, each pushing the other to evolve, innovate, and expand.

The Rivalry That Redefined Storytelling

This is more than a story of competition. It's the tale of how two companies, driven by ambition and passion, shaped an entire genre—and, in doing so, built universes that now span comics, films, games, and beyond.

The rivalry between DC and Marvel has not only entertained but also sparked debates, fueled fandoms, and created some of the most enduring characters in pop culture. It is a rivalry that has transcended industries, influencing everything from the art of storytelling to the technology of filmmaking.

But what truly sets this rivalry apart is that, in their quest for supremacy, DC and Marvel have ultimately elevated each other. Their competition has been a crucible of creativity, producing stories that inspire hope, courage, and the belief that heroes come in many forms.

Beyond Comics: A Multimedia Legacy

This book delves into the shared history and individual journeys of DC and Marvel, exploring not only their iconic characters but also their influence across industries:

- **Comics and Storytelling**: How their narratives reflect societal changes and cultural values.
- **Cinema and Streaming**: The battle for box office dominance and the evolution of superhero storytelling on platforms like HBO Max and Disney+.
- **Gaming and Interactivity**: How video games have expanded the superhero experience, offering fans a chance to step into their heroes' shoes.
- **Fandoms and Movements**: The passionate communities that have turned these universes into global cultural phenomena.
- **Merchandise and Branding**: The business strategies that transformed these stories into billion-dollar empires.

Why This Book?

This book isn't about picking sides—it's about celebrating the legacies of DC and Marvel, their shared impact on culture, and the creativity they've inspired across generations. Whether you're drawn to DC's mythic grandeur or Marvel's relatable heroes, this is a journey into the heart of what makes these universes so compelling.

What to Expect

From the golden age of comics to the age of streaming and digital media, we'll uncover how these two powerhouses have influenced not just each other but the entire entertainment landscape. Along the way, we'll celebrate the unity within the rivalry—a shared love for storytelling that reminds us why we need heroes.

Whether you've followed these universes for years or are just discovering them, this book invites you to explore their rich histories, their iconic characters, and their ever-evolving futures.

The adventure begins here, with a simple truth: the world is better with both DC and Marvel.

Chapter 1: Origins and Evolution

1.1 The Birth of DC: Where It All Began

In 1934, Major Malcolm Wheeler-Nicholson founded National Allied Publications, which would eventually become DC Comics. The company began humbly with pulp-style stories that combined action, mystery, and adventure. In 1938, they struck gold with ACTION COMICS #1, introducing Superman. This was more than a comic—it was a cultural event. Superman's instant popularity gave rise to the superhero genre, and within years, Batman (DETECTIVE COMICS #27) and Wonder Woman followed, cementing DC as a powerhouse of creativity.

DC's success wasn't just about characters; it was about pioneering ideas. They established what a superhero universe could be: a shared world where characters like Superman and Batman coexisted, creating the groundwork for the interconnected storytelling that would define comics.

1.2 Marvel's Humble Beginnings

Across town, in 1939, Martin Goodman founded Timely Comics. The company's first hero, the Human Torch, appeared in MARVEL COMICS #1 alongside Namor the Sub-Mariner. While these characters had their appeal, Marvel was still finding its identity. Unlike DC, Timely's heroes often lacked the larger-than-life personas that drew widespread attention.

By the 1950s, Timely evolved into Atlas Comics, producing a mix of genres, from horror to romance. But it wasn't until the early 1960s, when the company rebranded as Marvel Comics, that it truly revolutionized the industry.

1.3 The Silver Age Boom: Marvel's Explosive Growth

Marvel's renaissance began with Stan Lee, Jack Kirby, and Steve Ditko. Their groundbreaking approach introduced characters who were deeply human, facing real-world problems. Spider-Man was a teenager dealing with school bullies and guilt. The Fantastic Four were a bickering family navigating their newfound powers. Iron Man was a flawed billionaire grappling with his own mortality.

This era, known as the **Silver Age of Comics**, was marked by innovation and competition. DC, which had dominated for decades, suddenly had to contend with Marvel's dynamic, flawed, and relatable characters. Fans began to split into camps, debating whether Marvel's grounded stories were superior to DC's epic mythology.

1.4 The Industry Clash: Market Competition Heats Up

The 1970s and 1980s were a turning point. DC leaned into darker, more sophisticated storytelling, with landmark works like THE DARK KNIGHT RETURNS by Frank Miller and WATCHMEN by Alan Moore.

These stories redefined what superhero comics could be, delving into mature themes and pushing the boundaries of the medium.

Marvel, meanwhile, took bold risks of its own. Chris Claremont's X-MEN series became a cultural phenomenon, exploring themes of prejudice and identity. Characters like Wolverine, Storm, and Magneto became icons, and Marvel's ability to connect with younger audiences helped it dominate sales charts.

1.5 Defining Differences: Myth vs. Relatability

By the late 20th century, the fundamental differences between DC and Marvel became clear. DC's heroes were often seen as gods among men—idealized figures representing moral absolutes. Superman embodied hope, while Batman was the ultimate symbol of justice.

Marvel, in contrast, thrived on relatability. Their heroes were flawed individuals, grounded in real-life struggles. Peter Parker's financial woes, Tony Stark's struggles with addiction, and the X-Men's fight against discrimination made Marvel's universe feel closer to reality.

1.6 Expanding Universes: TV and Animation

Both companies recognized early on that their characters could thrive in other mediums. DC had a head start, with shows like THE ADVENTURES OF SUPERMAN in the 1950s and animated hits like SUPER FRIENDS in the 1970s. Marvel followed suit, producing iconic animated series such as SPIDER-MAN AND HIS AMAZING FRIENDS.

While DC's properties often leaned into lighthearted adventures, Marvel's shows aimed for a slightly edgier tone, reflecting the grittiness of their comics. These adaptations expanded the reach of both companies, attracting younger audiences and building fan loyalty.

1.7 The Modern Era: The Cinematic Prelude

The groundwork laid by their early successes eventually paved the way for Hollywood's superhero boom. DC scored early wins with SUPERMAN: THE MOVIE (1978) and BATMAN (1989), both of which proved that superhero films could be commercial and critical hits. Marvel struggled in the same era, licensing out its characters for often forgettable adaptations.

However, by the late 1990s, Marvel found its footing. Films like BLADE (1998) and X-MEN (2000) laid the foundation for the modern superhero blockbuster, setting the stage for the Marvel Cinematic Universe (MCU).

1.8 A Legacy of Innovation

Both companies have shaped not just comics but storytelling as a whole. DC introduced the world to the concept of the shared universe and defined what it meant to be a superhero. Marvel revolutionized the medium by proving that heroes could be as flawed and complex as the readers who loved them.

The rivalry that began with comics has grown into a cultural phenomenon, encompassing TV shows, movies, merchandise, and video games. Yet, despite their differences, DC and Marvel have always shared one thing: a commitment to inspiring audiences and telling unforgettable stories.

Chapter 2: Thematic Differences

2.1 The Mythic Legacy of DC

DC's heroes have long been regarded as mythic figures. Superman isn't just an alien with powers—he's a modern reinterpretation of Hercules, embodying the ideal of a savior. Wonder Woman channels the strength of Greek mythology, while Batman stands as a mortal who ascends to legendary status through willpower and intellect.

DC's stories often explore timeless themes like justice, sacrifice, and hope. These themes resonate because they tap into universal human experiences, elevating their characters to symbols of virtue and perseverance.

Examples:

- **The Justice League**: A pantheon of gods, representing humanity's collective aspirations.
- **Batman**: A mortal in a godlike world, proving that intellect and determination can rival any superpower.

2.2 Marvel's Relatable Approach

Marvel took a different path. Their heroes weren't gods or symbols—they were people, deeply flawed and inherently human. Spider-Man wasn't fighting for glory but to pay the bills and protect his loved ones. The X-Men struggled with societal rejection, echoing real-world issues like racism and discrimination.

Marvel's strength lies in its ability to make readers see themselves in its heroes. From Tony Stark's battle with addiction to Bruce Banner's uncontrollable rage, these characters remind us that imperfection is a part of being human.

Examples:

- **Spider-Man**: A teenager juggling heroism and high school life.
- **The X-Men**: A team that mirrors societal challenges, offering a reflection of real-world prejudice and the fight for equality.

2.3 World-Building: Fictional vs. Real Locations

One of the starkest contrasts between DC and Marvel lies in their settings.

- **DC's Fictional Cities**: Metropolis and Gotham are iconic, yet timeless. They represent ideals and fears rather than real-world locations. Metropolis is a city of hope, while Gotham is a noir-inspired world of corruption and decay.
- **Marvel's Real-World Integration**: Marvel grounds its stories in real cities. Spider-Man swings through the streets of New York, and the Avengers defend iconic landmarks. This choice makes Marvel's stories feel more immediate and accessible.

2.4 Villains: Ideologies vs. Flaws

Both universes boast incredible villains, but their approaches differ.

- **DC's Villains**: Often larger-than-life figures, embodying specific ideologies. The Joker is chaos personified, while Lex Luthor represents the dangers of unchecked ambition and intellect.
- **Marvel's Villains**: Often tragic figures, shaped by personal flaws or circumstances. Magneto fights for mutant survival, born of a

history of oppression. Doctor Octopus's genius becomes his downfall due to arrogance.

2.5 Themes of Teamwork and Solitude

- **DC**: Heroes often work alone, coming together only when the stakes are global. This solitary nature emphasizes their mythic qualities. Batman doesn't need help to save Gotham—he's a one-man army.

- **Marvel**: Collaboration is a recurring theme. The Avengers and X-Men demonstrate that teamwork, despite personal conflicts, is essential for overcoming larger threats.

2.6 Escaping the Human Condition vs. Embracing It

The philosophical divide between DC and Marvel runs deep:

- **DC's Heroes Escape the Human Condition**: Superman flies above the world's problems, inspiring people to reach higher. Wonder Woman comes from a utopia, showcasing what humanity could achieve.

- **Marvel's Heroes Embrace Humanity**: Their struggles with trauma, prejudice, and personal failings make them more relatable and grounded.

2.7 Storytelling Structures

- **DC**: Frequently uses archetypal storytelling, with heroes overcoming monumental trials that echo ancient epics.

- **Marvel**: Leans into serialized narratives, where characters grow and change over time. Peter Parker grows up, marries, and experiences loss, creating a continuous, evolving story.

2.8 Cultural Impact of These Themes

Thematic differences have influenced their cultural reach. DC's archetypal heroes often inspire larger-than-life adaptations, from the grandeur of SUPERMAN: THE MOVIE to THE DARK KNIGHT TRILOGY. Marvel's relatable approach has fostered a cinematic universe where individual stories weave into a grand tapestry.

2.9 The Evolution of Themes Over Time

- **Golden Age (1930s–1940s)**:
    - DC: Emphasis on hope and moral absolutism in a post-Depression, pre-WWII world (e.g., Superman fighting for "Truth, Justice, and the American Way").
    - Marvel: Initially focusing on pulp adventures, with some early anti-fascist themes through characters like Captain America.

- **Silver Age (1950s–1960s)**:
    - DC: Transition to science fiction and high-concept storytelling, reflecting the Space Race.
    - Marvel: Tackled social issues like racism and youth rebellion (e.g., X-Men as a metaphor for civil rights struggles).

- **Modern Era (2000s–Present):**
    - DC: Darker and introspective tones, with heroes questioning their roles in an imperfect world (WATCHMEN's legacy).
    - Marvel: Balance of humor, action, and social commentary (e.g., BLACK PANTHER addressing systemic racism).

2.10 Cross-Cultural Appeal

- Analyze how themes translate globally:
    - Superman as a universal symbol of hope.
    - Spider-Man's relatability transcending cultural barriers.

2.11 Subversion of Heroic Tropes

- DC: KINGDOM COME and INJUSTICE explore dystopian futures where heroes fail or turn corrupt.
- Marvel: The CIVIL WAR storyline challenges the concept of heroism through ideological conflict.

Chapter 3: Iconic Characters Showdown

3.1 Superman vs. Thor: Godlike Beings in Different Contexts

- **Deeper Analysis of Superman**: The weight of his dual identity as Clark Kent and Kal-El. Superman represents what humanity aspires to be, often wrestling with his role as Earth's savior while longing for the simplicity of human life.

- **Deeper Analysis of Thor**: Thor's arc in mythology and comics. While Superman's moral compass is unshakable, Thor struggles with arrogance, learning humility over time.

- **Narrative Impact**: Both characters often face cosmic threats but differ in how they resolve conflicts—Superman through diplomacy and raw power, Thor through battle and camaraderie.

3.2 Batman vs. Iron Man: The Battle of Billionaires

- **Batman's Tactics**: His reliance on fear, his detective skills, and his unmatched preparation for any scenario. Highlight his relationships with villains like the Joker, which test his moral boundaries.

- **Iron Man's Vulnerability**: Tony Stark's struggles with addiction, PTSD, and his ego. Unlike Batman, who hides in shadows, Stark's heroism is public and flamboyant, making him a polarizing figure.

- **Philosophical Differences**: While Batman fights crime to avenge his parents, Stark sees heroism as redemption for his past mistakes, particularly the weapons his company created.

3.3 Wonder Woman vs. Captain Marvel: Female Empowerment Icons

- **Wonder Woman's Role**: Explore her origin as an Amazon warrior, crafted to bridge the gap between gods and humans. Her stories often challenge patriarchy and celebrate compassion.

- **Captain Marvel's Evolution**: From a supporting character to a central figure in Marvel, Carol Danvers represents empowerment in a contemporary context, battling systemic challenges and intergalactic foes.

- **Impact on Gender Representation**: Compare how each character has influenced perceptions of female heroes in comics, films, and beyond.

3.4 Flash vs. Spider-Man: The Speedster and the Wall-Crawler

- **Flash's Legacy**: Multiple characters (Barry Allen, Wally West) have taken the mantle of the Flash, making it a story of legacy and perseverance.

- **Spider-Man's Responsibility**: Peter Parker's motto, "With great power comes great responsibility," underscores his entire arc. His struggles with balancing personal life and heroism resonate deeply with readers.

- **Youthful Energy and Humor**: Both characters bring levity to their universes, with Flash's quips and Spider-Man's witty banter offering a break from darker narratives.

3.5 Justice League vs. Avengers: Team Dynamics

- **Justice League's Unity**: Formed to tackle godlike threats, the Justice League often operates as a symbol of global unity. Highlight key storylines like CRISIS ON INFINITE EARTHS and THE NEW FRONTIER.

- **Avengers' Complexity**: The Avengers are often dysfunctional, driven by interpersonal conflicts. Their strength lies in their diversity, with characters like Hulk, Black Widow, and Captain America bringing different strengths to the table.

- **Team Leadership**: Compare Batman and Superman's leadership styles with Captain America and Iron Man's approaches.

3.6 Antiheroes and Dark Figures

- **DC's Antiheroes**: Expand on Constantine's role as a morally ambiguous character, navigating the supernatural, and Lobo's chaotic, violent escapades.

- **Marvel's Antiheroes**: Delve into Wolverine's tortured past and Deadpool's meta-humor, both of which redefine traditional heroism.

- **Cultural Reception**: Discuss how audiences perceive antiheroes and their growing popularity in modern storytelling.

3.7 Villains Who Define Heroes

- **Lex Luthor vs. Doctor Doom**: Two genius villains who often mirror their respective heroes, Superman and Reed Richards.

- **Joker vs. Green Goblin**: Both represent chaos and unpredictability, targeting their heroes' deepest fears.
- **Magneto vs. Darkseid**: The ideological villain (Magneto) vs. the embodiment of evil (Darkseid).

3.8 The Influence of Iconic Characters

- **Merchandising and Pop Culture**: How characters like Batman and Spider-Man dominate sales of toys, apparel, and media.
- **Adaptations Across Mediums**: Discuss major portrayals in film, TV, and video games, such as Kevin Conroy's Batman or Tobey Maguire's Spider-Man.
- **Crossover Potential**: Explore how fans fantasize about DC and Marvel heroes interacting, emphasizing their similarities and contrasts.

3.9 Lesser-Known Heroes Who Shaped the Universes

- DC: Swamp Thing, Animal Man, and Zatanna as cult-favorite characters who explore unique themes (environmentalism, magic).
- Marvel: Moon Knight, Ms. Marvel, and Shang-Chi bring diversity and fresh storytelling styles to the forefront.

3.10 Supporting Characters and Sidekicks

- DC's Robin and Alfred as essential to Batman's narrative arc.
- Marvel's Pepper Potts, Bucky Barnes, and Happy Hogan as integral to humanizing its larger-than-life heroes.

3.11 Rivalries Within Teams

- DC: Batman vs. Superman in ideological debates over justice and morality (JUSTICE LEAGUE dynamics).

- Marvel: Internal Avengers conflicts, such as Iron Man's pragmatism clashing with Captain America's idealism.

Chapter 4: The Cinematic Rivalry

4.9 The Role of Casting in Shaping Legacy

The choice of actors has been pivotal in defining DC and Marvel's cinematic identities.

- **DC's Icons**: Christopher Reeve became synonymous with Superman, while Christian Bale redefined Batman with his grounded and intense portrayal. Gal Gadot's Wonder Woman brought grace and strength, earning widespread acclaim.

- **Marvel's Breakthroughs**: Robert Downey Jr.'s Iron Man launched the MCU, while Chris Evans' Captain America became the embodiment of heroism. Casting lesser-known actors, like Tom Hiddleston as Loki, allowed Marvel to redefine characters for new audiences.

4.10 Cinematic Technology and Innovations

Both universes have pushed the boundaries of film technology:

- **DC's Visual Style**: Zack Snyder's use of slow-motion, hyper-realistic CGI, and desaturated palettes created a unique, albeit divisive, aesthetic.

- **Marvel's Spectacle**: The MCU embraced cutting-edge motion capture and CGI, particularly in films like AVENGERS: INFINITY WAR, where Thanos became a fully-realized character through Josh Brolin's performance.

- **IMAX and 3D**: Both franchises utilized these technologies to enhance the cinematic experience, with DC's THE DARK KNIGHT being one of the first blockbusters to heavily incorporate IMAX.

4.11 Marketing and Fan Engagement

- **DC's Prestige Marketing**: Focused on building hype around key events like the release of THE SNYDER CUT, DC often relied on exclusivity and fan campaigns.

- **Marvel's Grassroots Hype**: Marvel mastered teaser culture, using post-credit scenes and viral campaigns to keep audiences excited for future films.

4.12 Critical Reception: A Tale of Two Studios

While Marvel often strikes a balance between critical and commercial success, DC's reception has been more polarizing.

- **Marvel's Formula**: Known for consistent quality, humor, and emotional depth. Films like BLACK PANTHER were critically celebrated for their cultural significance.

- **DC's Highs and Lows**: Projects like JOKER (2019) and THE BATMAN (2022) received critical acclaim, but missteps like SUICIDE SQUAD (2016) hurt the brand's reputation.

4.13 Television as a Battleground

- **DC's Dominance on TV**: Shows like ARROW, THE FLASH, and SMALLVILLE established DC as a television juggernaut, focusing on serialized storytelling and character development.

- **Marvel's Streaming Success**: The MCU expanded to Disney+ with interconnected series like WANDAVISION and LOKI, enhancing its cinematic universe.

4.14 Global Influence and Fandom

- **DC's Timeless Appeal**: Characters like Superman and Batman are universally recognized, often associated with American ideals of hope and justice.

- **Marvel's Modern Resonance**: The MCU's diverse cast and global narratives have helped it resonate with audiences worldwide, particularly younger generations.

4.15 Lessons Learned and Future Challenges

Both franchises have evolved, learning from past mistakes:

- **DC's Focus on Quality Over Quantity**: Recent projects emphasize standalone excellence, with films like THE BATMAN prioritizing storytelling over universe-building.

- **Marvel's Expansion Risks**: The MCU's ambitious multiverse saga carries the challenge of maintaining coherence and audience investment.

4.16 Marketing as a Cinematic Weapon

- **DC**: Use of cryptic trailers and viral campaigns (THE DARK KNIGHT'S "Why So Serious?" ARG).

- **Marvel**: Post-credit scenes as a hook for future films, creating a perpetual cycle of hype.

4.17 Evolution of Visual Effects

- **DC**: Snyder's signature use of slow-motion and epic, painterly visuals.

- **Marvel**: The seamless integration of motion-capture performances like Josh Brolin's Thanos in INFINITY WAR.

4.18 The Role of Music

- **DC**: Iconic scores like John Williams' SUPERMAN THEME and Hans Zimmer's THE DARK KNIGHT score.

- **Marvel**: Alan Silvestri's AVENGERS THEME becoming synonymous with superhero teamwork.

Chapter 5: Fan Cultures

5.7 Fandom in the Era of Streaming

Streaming services have revolutionized how fans consume content, fostering new communities.

- **Binge-Watching Culture**: Shows like THE FLASH (CW) and DAREDEVIL (Netflix) allow fans to immerse themselves in superhero narratives for hours.

- **Fan Forums and Analysis**: Platforms like YouTube and Twitch are filled with in-depth episode breakdowns, character analyses, and live reaction videos, further enhancing fan engagement.

5.8 The Role of Merchandise in Fandom

Merchandise plays a critical role in fandom identity.

- **Wearable Allegiances**: Fans express their loyalty through clothing, accessories, and cosplay outfits featuring logos like the Bat-Symbol or Captain America's shield.

- **Collectibles and Action Figures**: Limited-edition items become prized possessions, fueling a thriving secondary market.

- **Video Games**: Titles like ARKHAM ASYLUM (DC) and SPIDER-MAN (Marvel) provide interactive experiences, deepening fans' connection to these universes.

5.9 Cross-Fandom Creativity

Some fans transcend the rivalry by creating works that unite both universes.

- **Crossover Fan Fiction**: Stories where Batman teams up with Spider-Man or Wonder Woman faces off against Thor showcase the creativity of fans imagining shared universes.

- **Custom Art and Mashups**: Artists frequently blend styles and characters, creating unique interpretations that celebrate both franchises.

5.10 Fan Debates and "What-If" Scenarios

Debates over hypothetical matchups fuel fan interaction.

- **Forums and Polls**: Questions like "Who would win: Superman or Thor?" generate thousands of responses and passionate arguments.

- **Fan-Made Battles**: Animators and creators on platforms like YouTube produce cinematic battles, giving fans visual representations of these epic "What-If" scenarios.

5.11 The Positive Power of Fandom

Beyond competition, these fandoms inspire collaboration and charity:

- **Fundraising Efforts**: Groups like the SNYDER CUT MOVEMENT raised funds for suicide prevention, showing the power of fans to make a positive impact.

- **Community-Building**: Events like cosplay gatherings and fan conventions create spaces for inclusivity and shared passion.

5.12 Future of Fan Culture

As technology advances, fan culture will evolve in exciting ways:

- **Virtual Reality**: Fans may soon explore Metropolis or swing through New York as Spider-Man in fully immersive VR experiences.

- **Augmented Reality (AR)**: Apps that let fans project superheroes into their living spaces or interact with their favorite characters in real time.

- **Global Connectivity**: More fans from different cultural backgrounds will bring unique perspectives to the DC vs. Marvel debate, enriching the conversation.

5.13 Generational Divide in Fandoms

- Older fans gravitate toward DC's mythic storytelling, while younger audiences embrace Marvel's humor and relatability.

5.14 Social Media's Role in Shaping Fandom

- Platforms like Reddit, TikTok, and YouTube create echo chambers for DC vs. Marvel debates.

- Fan edits and mashups become a form of creative expression.

5.15 Fan Campaigns and Movements

- THE SNYDER CUT MOVEMENT as an example of fans influencing corporate decisions.

- Marvel fans advocating for underrepresented characters like the Young Avengers.

Chapter 6: Collaboration and Crossovers

6.6 Uniting Creative Talent

Collaborations between DC and Marvel didn't just involve their characters—they also brought together some of the best creative minds in the industry.

- **Creators at the Helm**: Writers and artists like George Pérez, John Byrne, and Walt Simonson worked on crossover projects, blending their unique styles to bring these universes together.

- **Artistic Challenges**: Crafting visuals that harmonized two distinct aesthetics—DC's mythic grandeur and Marvel's grounded relatability—was a daunting yet rewarding task.

6.7 Unofficial Crossovers and Easter Eggs

Even when formal collaborations were rare, subtle nods and winks often connected the two universes:

- **Parodic Crossovers**: Independent creators and smaller publishers occasionally created unofficial works poking fun at the rivalry.

- **Easter Eggs in Comics**: Look for cheeky nods like a character reading a rival's comic or background posters hinting at cross-universe heroes.

6.8 Collaborative Opportunities Beyond Fiction

Collaborations extend beyond traditional storytelling:

- **Educational Campaigns**: Both companies have occasionally participated in broader initiatives, using their characters to promote literacy, anti-bullying, and public health campaigns.

- **Charity Events**: Joint charity auctions featuring art and memorabilia have united fans for a good cause, highlighting the potential for collaboration outside of comics.

6.9 The Concept of "What-If" Universes

The idea of multiverses has grown in popularity in recent years, leading fans to wonder how DC and Marvel could coexist within such a framework.

- **Incorporating the Multiverse Concept**: Both universes now feature multiverse storylines, with Marvel's WHAT IF...? series and DC's CRISIS ON INFINITE EARTHS. Theoretically, these concepts could allow for a crossover without compromising either franchise's integrity.

- **Fan-Driven Crossovers**: Online forums and discussions are filled with imaginative ideas for multiverse-spanning adventures that blend the two worlds.

6.10 The Impact on Fandoms

Crossovers are often polarizing within fan communities:

- **Excitement and Nostalgia**: Longtime fans celebrate these events as rare opportunities to see their favorite characters interact.

- **Criticism of Execution**: Some fans believe crossovers dilute the unique qualities of each universe, making the stories feel less authentic.

6.11 The Legacy of Crossovers

Despite their rarity, crossovers remain a significant part of comic book history, symbolizing what can be achieved when rivalries are set aside for creative collaboration.

- **Inspiration for Future Stories**: These collaborations have inspired countless homages, spinoffs, and even real-world collaborations between creators.

- **A Symbol of Unity**: They remind readers and creators alike that at the heart of both DC and Marvel lies a shared love for storytelling.

Chapter 7: The Business Side

7.1 The Origins of the Business Rivalry

DC and Marvel didn't just compete creatively; their rivalry extended to the business world, where they fought for market share and dominance.

- **Early Dominance of DC**: In the Golden and Silver Ages, DC held a significant lead in sales and cultural influence. Titles like ACTION COMICS and DETECTIVE COMICS were household staples.

- **Marvel's Disruption**: In the 1960s, Marvel revolutionized comics with relatable heroes, capturing younger audiences and rapidly increasing its market share.

7.2 Publishing Wars

The two companies constantly sought ways to outmaneuver each other in the publishing space.

- **DC's Expansion**: In the 1980s, DC acquired smaller publishers like Charlton and Milestone, integrating characters such as the Blue Beetle and Static Shock into its universe.

- **Marvel's Countermoves**: Marvel innovated with series like WHAT IF...?, focusing on alternate takes and niche audiences, and dominated the 1990s with X-Men-related titles.

7.3 The Bankruptcy That Shook Marvel

In the mid-1990s, Marvel faced bankruptcy, forced to sell the film and merchandising rights for many of its characters, including Spider-Man and the X-Men.

- **Impact of Licensing**: This decision allowed other studios, like Sony and Fox, to produce Marvel films but also fractured Marvel's cinematic ambitions.

- **The Rebound**: Marvel's recovery began in the early 2000s with its own film studio, culminating in the MCU's launch with IRON MAN in 2008.

7.4 DC and Warner Bros.: A Partnership of Power

Since the 1960s, DC has been a subsidiary of Warner Bros., giving it access to one of the largest entertainment platforms in the world.

- **Advantages of Warner Bros.**: DC benefited from the resources and reach of a major studio, leading to iconic adaptations like BATMAN: THE ANIMATED SERIES and Christopher Nolan's THE DARK KNIGHT.

- **Challenges of Corporate Oversight**: However, creative clashes between filmmakers and executives often led to inconsistent visions in the DCEU.

7.5 The Merchandise Battle

The competition wasn't limited to comics and films; merchandise became a battleground as well.

- **DC's Collectibles**: DC leveraged its timeless icons, producing high-quality action figures, graphic novels, and apparel featuring Batman, Superman, and Wonder Woman.

- **Marvel's Toys and Games**: Marvel excelled in branding, licensing its characters for toys, video games, and crossover promotions with brands like LEGO.

7.6 Global Reach and Branding

Both companies expanded their influence globally, tailoring their strategies to international audiences.

- **DC's Global Icons**: Characters like Superman and Batman became universal symbols, transcending language and culture.

- **Marvel's Pop Culture Dominance**: Marvel's diverse characters and humorous tone appealed to younger, global audiences, especially through the MCU.

7.7 The Streaming Era

The rise of streaming services brought new challenges and opportunities.

- **DC's Strategy**: DC launched its own streaming service, DC Universe, offering exclusive shows like TITANS and DOOM PATROL before transitioning to HBO Max.

- **Marvel's Dominance on Disney+**: Marvel capitalized on Disney's vast platform, releasing interconnected series like WANDAVISION and LOKI.

7.8 Box Office Battles

Both studios have made billions from superhero films, but their approaches differ.

- **DC's High-Risk, High-Reward Strategy**: Films like JOKER and THE BATMAN focused on auteur-driven narratives, earning critical acclaim and massive profits.

- **Marvel's Consistency**: The MCU's interconnected universe ensured steady box office success, with AVENGERS: ENDGAME becoming one of the highest-grossing films ever.

7.9 Video Games as a Revenue Stream

- **DC's Successes**: The BATMAN: ARKHAM series set a new standard for superhero games, offering deep storytelling and innovative gameplay.

- **Marvel's Growth**: Titles like MARVEL'S SPIDER-MAN on PlayStation have helped Marvel establish itself as a serious contender in gaming.

7.10 The Future of the Business Rivalry

- **DC's Reorganization**: With James Gunn and Peter Safran taking creative leadership, DC aims to streamline its cinematic and storytelling vision.

- **Marvel's Expansions**: The MCU continues to grow with its Multiverse Saga, incorporating new characters and exploring diverse genres.

Chapter 8: The Evolution of Art and Design

8.1 The Golden Age: Establishing the Iconic Look

The 1930s and 1940s set the foundation for comic art, with simple yet bold designs that emphasized clarity and heroism.

- **DC's Early Aesthetic**:
    - Artists like Joe Shuster (SUPERMAN) and Bob Kane (BATMAN) focused on clean lines and bright colors to evoke optimism.
    - Costumes were designed to be striking yet functional, with Superman's "S" shield becoming a symbol of hope.

- **Marvel's Beginnings**:
    - Marvel's early designs leaned heavily on pulp magazine influences, with dramatic shading and exaggerated poses.
    - Characters like Namor and the Human Torch had a raw, adventurous feel.

8.2 The Silver Age: A Revolution in Style

The Silver Age (1950s–1960s) brought dynamic compositions and experimental panel layouts.

- **DC's Streamlined Look**:
    - Artists like Carmine Infantino introduced sleek, futuristic designs (THE FLASH), emphasizing speed and fluidity.

- o   The art became more vibrant, reflecting the optimism of the Space Race era.

- **Marvel's Energetic Style:**

    - o   Jack Kirby's work redefined comic art with bold, kinetic lines and larger-than-life visuals (FANTASTIC FOUR, THOR).

    - o   Steve Ditko introduced surreal, otherworldly designs in DOCTOR STRANGE and the expressive, relatable world of SPIDER-MAN.

8.3 The Bronze Age: Grit and Realism

From the 1970s to 1980s, comic art took on darker tones to reflect societal changes.

- **DC's Darker Shift:**

    - o   Artists like Neal Adams brought realism to titles like BATMAN, emphasizing anatomy and shadow for a noir-like effect.

    - o   Experimental works, such as SWAMP THING by Bernie Wrightson, showcased atmospheric and gothic aesthetics.

- **Marvel's Bold Realism:**

    - o   Artists like John Romita Sr. (SPIDER-MAN) and Frank Miller (DAREDEVIL) used dramatic contrasts and gritty textures to depict urban environments.

    - o   The rise of graphic novels, such as THE DEATH OF CAPTAIN MARVEL, allowed for more artistic freedom.

8.4 The Modern Era: Digital Innovation and Cinematic Influence

The 1990s and 2000s saw a revolution in comic art with digital tools transforming the medium.

- **DC's Cinematic Style**:
    - Titles like KINGDOM COME (art by Alex Ross) brought hyper-realistic, painted artwork to the forefront, blending fine art with comic storytelling.
    - Digital tools allowed for more detailed backgrounds and dynamic effects, elevating flagship series like JUSTICE LEAGUE.

- **Marvel's Technological Leap**:
    - Artists like Jim Lee (X-MEN) and Mark Bagley (ULTIMATE SPIDER-MAN) used bold, intricate linework enhanced by digital coloring.
    - Cross-media influences brought cinematic framing to comics, reflecting the rise of the MCU.

8.5 The Role of Color and Typography

Color and typography have played pivotal roles in shaping each universe's identity:

- **DC's Color Palette**: Often uses high contrast and symbolic hues (e.g., Superman's red and blue for hope, Batman's dark tones for mystery).

- **Marvel's Expressive Typography**: Titles like AMAZING SPIDER-MAN feature dynamic fonts that match the character's energy and tone.

8.6 Art Beyond the Page: Merchandise and Marketing

- **DC's Branding**: The Bat-Symbol and Superman's "S" logo became iconic not only in comics but in global merchandise.
- **Marvel's Expansion**: Characters like Iron Man and the Avengers were reimagined in stylized designs for toys, video games, and apparel.

8.7 The Future of Comic Art

With evolving technology, both DC and Marvel are pushing boundaries in art and design:

- **Virtual Reality Comics**: Interactive storytelling that allows readers to explore Gotham or Wakanda in immersive detail.
- **AI-Assisted Art**: Using AI to enhance backgrounds and textures while preserving the artist's unique style.
- **Augmented Reality (AR) Features**: Comics with QR codes that unlock animated panels or bonus content.

8.8 Iconic Artists and Their Lasting Impact

Exploring the contributions of individual artists who left an indelible mark on their respective universes:

- **DC's Legends**:

    o Alex Ross (KINGDOM COME, SUPERMAN: PEACE ON EARTH): His hyper-realistic, painterly style elevated superhero art to fine art status.

    o Jim Lee (BATMAN: HUSH, JUSTICE LEAGUE): Known for dynamic poses and intricate linework, defining the modern DC aesthetic.

- **Marvel's Visionaries**:

    o John Byrne (X-MEN, FANTASTIC FOUR): His clean, classic style was integral in shaping Marvel's Golden Age storytelling.

    o Mike Deodato Jr. (AVENGERS, SPIDER-MAN): His dark, dramatic tones added depth to Marvel's 1990s comics.

8.9 The Role of Women in Comic Art

Highlighting female artists and their contributions to the industry:

- **DC's Trailblazers**: Nicola Scott (WONDER WOMAN, BIRDS OF PREY) and Jen Bartel (HARLEY QUINN) brought bold, empowering visuals to iconic female characters.

- **Marvel's Innovators**: Artists like Sara Pichelli (MILES MORALES: SPIDER-MAN) redefined how modern heroes are presented, focusing on diversity and youthful energy.

8.10 Experimental Art Styles and Indie Influences

Both DC and Marvel occasionally embraced experimental styles, inspired by indie comics:

- **DC's Avant-Garde Projects**:

    - SANDMAN (Vertigo): Blended surrealism and fantasy, influencing mainstream DC titles.

    - BATMAN: BLACK AND WHITE: Used stark monochromatic visuals to explore darker, psychological narratives.

- **Marvel's Stylized Runs**:

    - MARVELS (Alex Ross) explored everyday life through the eyes of ordinary people, blending realism with storytelling.

    - HAWKEYE (David Aja): Minimalistic, graphic art style that emphasized humor and character interactions.

8.11 Crossovers and Design Synergy

The collaborative spirit of crossovers also influenced art styles:

- DC VS. MARVEL: Artists had to blend the visual styles of both universes seamlessly.

- AMALGAM UNIVERSE: Designs like Dark Claw (Batman + Wolverine) combined the iconic traits of both characters into cohesive new looks.

8.12 How Comics Influence Other Media

Comic art isn't confined to the page—it heavily impacts other forms of entertainment:

- **Animated Series**:
    - DC's BATMAN: THE ANIMATED SERIES adopted a neo-noir, art deco aesthetic, setting the standard for superhero cartoons.
    - Marvel's X-MEN: THE ANIMATED SERIES used bold, energetic designs that mirrored its comic origins.

- **Live-Action Films**:
    - Storyboarding for films often relies on comic panels, using their dynamic compositions as blueprints (300 and SIN CITY as notable examples).

Chapter 9: Video Games and Interactive Media

9.1 Early Adventures: The Rise of Superheroes in Gaming

Superheroes entered the gaming world in the 1980s, beginning with arcade and 8-bit console games.

- **DC's First Forays**:

    - SUPERMAN (Atari 2600, 1979): One of the first superhero games, offering a simple yet iconic gaming experience.

    - BATMAN: THE CAPED CRUSADER (1988): Blended adventure and puzzle-solving, laying the groundwork for more complex superhero games.

- **Marvel's Early Hits**:

    - SPIDER-MAN (Atari 2600, 1982): Focused on climbing skyscrapers and battling Green Goblin.

    - X-MEN: MADNESS IN MURDERWORLD (1989): A text-based adventure showcasing Marvel's storytelling focus.

9.2 The Golden Age of Superhero Gaming (1990s–2000s)

The 1990s saw rapid advancements in gaming technology, bringing superheroes to life in richer detail.

- **DC's Golden Era:**

    - THE ADVENTURES OF BATMAN & ROBIN (1994): Captured the art deco aesthetics of the animated series.

    - JUSTICE LEAGUE TASK FORCE (1995): A fighting game featuring DC's most iconic heroes.

- **Marvel's Expansion:**

    - X-MEN: CHILDREN OF THE ATOM (1994): Introduced Marvel characters into the arcade fighting genre.

    - SPIDER-MAN (2000): A landmark game that allowed players to swing freely through New York City.

9.3 The Modern Renaissance of Superhero Games

The 2010s ushered in a new era of superhero gaming, defined by high-quality, story-driven experiences.

- **DC's Triumphs:**

    - BATMAN: ARKHAM ASYLUM (2009) revolutionized superhero gaming with its fluid combat system, detective mechanics, and dark narrative.

    - INJUSTICE: GODS AMONG US (2013) brought DC heroes into the fighting game genre, incorporating a gripping alternate universe storyline.

- **Marvel's Comeback:**

    - MARVEL'S SPIDER-MAN (2018): An open-world masterpiece praised for its emotional depth and thrilling gameplay.

- o MARVEL'S AVENGERS (2020): Attempted to replicate the MCU's ensemble dynamic, though it received mixed reviews.

9.4 Mobile Games and Casual Engagement

Mobile gaming expanded accessibility to superhero content.

- **DC's Mobile Hits**:
    - o DC LEGENDS and INJUSTICE MOBILE allowed players to collect and battle heroes on the go.
- **Marvel's Mobile Success**:
    - o MARVEL: CONTEST OF CHAMPIONS became a global phenomenon with its roster of characters and competitive gameplay.

9.5 VR and AR Innovations

Virtual and augmented reality have brought new ways for fans to engage with superheroes.

- **DC's Experiments**: VR experiences like BATMAN: ARKHAM VR allowed players to step into the Dark Knight's cowl.
- **Marvel's AR Apps**: Interactive apps let fans project characters into their environment or explore augmented reality comic panels.

9.6 Collaborative and Online Games

Online multiplayer games brought superheroes together in shared universes:

- **DC Universe Online (2011)**: An MMORPG that let players create custom heroes and fight alongside the Justice League.

- **Marvel Heroes (2013)**: An action-RPG featuring fan-favorite characters, fostering a sense of community among players.

9.7 The Business of Gaming: Licensing and Branding

Video games became a lucrative revenue stream for both companies:

- **DC's Partnerships**: Collaborated with studios like Rocksteady (ARKHAM series) to deliver AAA experiences.

- **Marvel's Strategy**: Partnered with Sony for exclusive titles like SPIDER-MAN, ensuring high production values.

9.8 The Future of Superhero Gaming

Both universes are poised to redefine gaming with upcoming releases:

- **DC's Future Projects**:
    - SUICIDE SQUAD: KILL THE JUSTICE LEAGUE promises a mix of humor and dark storytelling.

- **Marvel's New Horizons**:
    - MARVEL'S WOLVERINE and MIDNIGHT SUNS continue to diversify Marvel's gaming portfolio.

9.9 Niche and Indie Superhero Games

Not all superhero games are blockbuster productions; smaller studios and indie developers have also explored the genre:

- **DC's Experiments**:
    - Spin-off titles like GOTHAM CITY IMPOSTORS (2012) provided a comedic, multiplayer take on Gotham's vigilante culture.

- **Marvel's Hidden Gems**:
    - Indie-inspired games like DEADPOOL (2013) broke the fourth wall, offering fans a unique, self-aware experience.

9.10 Esports and Competitive Gaming

Superhero games have entered the esports arena, with competitive communities forming around certain titles:

- **DC in Esports**:
    - INJUSTICE 2 became a staple in fighting game tournaments, showcasing DC's rich roster of heroes and villains.

- **Marvel in Esports**:
    - The MARVEL VS. CAPCOM series has long been a favorite in the fighting game community, celebrated for its high-speed action and flashy combos.

9.11 The Role of Narrative in Superhero Games

Modern superhero games are as much about storytelling as they are about gameplay:

- **DC's Narrative Focus:**
    - The ARKHAM series redefined how games could tell a deep, character-driven story, delving into Batman's psyche.

- **Marvel's Narrative Approach:**
    - MARVEL'S SPIDER-MAN combined action with emotional storytelling, such as Peter Parker's relationships and sacrifices.

9.12 Games as Canon Extensions

Some superhero games are considered part of their respective universes, offering canonical or semi-canonical stories:

- **DC's Canonical Games:**
    - INJUSTICE: GODS AMONG US introduced an alternate timeline that later expanded into a successful comic series.

- **Marvel's Tie-Ins:**
    - SPIDER-MAN (PS4) is considered a standalone universe within the Marvel multiverse, influencing fan theories about potential cinematic crossovers.

9.13 The Role of Music and Sound Design in Superhero Games

Soundtracks and audio play a critical role in immersing players in the superhero experience:

- **DC's Atmospheric Scores**:
    - The brooding, orchestral themes in ARKHAM ASYLUM emphasized Gotham's dark, ominous tone.
- **Marvel's Energetic Soundtracks**:
    - The upbeat and heroic music in MARVEL'S SPIDER-MAN mirrors the character's optimistic and energetic personality.

9.14 Expanding Accessibility in Gaming

Both companies have worked to make their games more inclusive:

- **DC's Accessibility Innovations**:
    - Features like customizable controls in GOTHAM KNIGHTS made gameplay more accessible to players with disabilities.
- **Marvel's Focus on Diversity**:
    - Games like MILES MORALES highlight diverse heroes, ensuring representation extends to interactive media.

Chapter 10: The Business of Licensing and Merchandise

10.1 The Rise of Superhero Merchandising

Merchandising began as a supplemental revenue stream but quickly became a cornerstone of superhero franchises.

- **DC's Early Efforts**:
    - In the 1940s, Superman lunchboxes and Batman capes introduced the concept of superhero-themed products for children.
    - The 1960s BATMAN TV show with Adam West fueled a boom in DC-themed toys and costumes.

- **Marvel's Beginnings**:
    - The 1960s saw Marvel experimenting with tie-in products, such as SPIDER-MAN action figures and branded school supplies.

10.2 The Golden Age of Action Figures

The 1980s and 1990s marked the heyday of superhero action figures, driven by major licensing deals.

- **DC's Partnerships**:
    - Collaborated with Kenner to produce the iconic SUPER POWERS COLLECTION in the 1980s, which featured highly articulated figures with unique action features.

- **Marvel's Growth in Toys**:
    - Partnered with Toy Biz to launch extensive lines of X-Men and Spider-Man figures in the 1990s, capitalizing on their animated series' popularity.

10.3 Clothing, Apparel, and Everyday Branding

Superhero logos became fashion staples, transcending comic book culture:

- **DC's Iconography**:
    - The Bat-Symbol and Superman's "S" shield became universal emblems of heroism, frequently used on t-shirts, hats, and backpacks.

- **Marvel's Casual Appeal**:
    - Quirky slogans like "With Great Power Comes Great Responsibility" from Spider-Man adorned countless products, appealing to younger audiences.

10.4 Collectibles and High-End Merchandise

As comic book fandom matured, so did the demand for premium collectibles:

- **DC's High-End Market**:
    - Limited-edition statues of Batman, Wonder Woman, and the Joker became staples for adult collectors.
    - HOT TOYS partnerships produced highly detailed, poseable figures tied to the DCEU.

- **Marvel's Premium Collectibles**:
    - Companies like Sideshow Collectibles released intricate replicas of Iron Man suits and Avengers dioramas, appealing to high-income fans.

10.5 The Role of Comic-Con in Merchandise

Events like San Diego Comic-Con became pivotal for showcasing and launching exclusive products:

- **DC Exclusives**:
    - Comic-Con often featured limited-edition comics, toys, and statues, such as holographic covers of Superman comics or collectible Batman busts.
- **Marvel Exclusives**:
    - Limited-edition items, such as signed lithographs and variant covers, became a major draw for Marvel collectors.

10.6 Video Games and Digital Merchandise

Gaming has expanded into a significant revenue stream for superhero merchandise:

- **DC's Integration**:
    - INJUSTICE 2 offered downloadable content (DLC), including alternate costumes and exclusive characters, driving additional revenue.

- **Marvel's Innovations:**
    - MARVEL'S SPIDER-MAN introduced pre-order bonuses tied to in-game outfits, incentivizing early purchases.

10.7 NFTs and the Digital Future

The rise of NFTs has introduced new opportunities for superhero branding:

- **DC's Foray into NFTs:**
    - Launched digital collectibles featuring Batman and Superman, offering fans unique ownership experiences.

- **Marvel's Digital Collectibles:**
    - Partnered with VeVe to release NFTs based on classic comic covers and iconic characters.

10.8 The Global Licensing Battle

Superheroes became a global phenomenon, leading to regional adaptations of merchandise:

- **DC's International Reach:**
    - Batman and Superman-themed products, such as bicycles and lunchboxes, were tailored to different markets, with localized branding.

- **Marvel's Localization Efforts**:
    - Created products featuring characters like Shang-Chi and Kamala Khan, appealing to Asian and Middle Eastern audiences.

10.9 The Evolution of Licensing Strategies

Over the decades, DC and Marvel have continuously refined their licensing models to maximize reach:

- **DC's Early Licensing Moves**:
    - In the 1970s, DC partnered with consumer goods companies to create Superman-branded cereal boxes and Batman lunch kits.

- **Marvel's Growth Through Licensing**:
    - Marvel's licensing deals in the 1990s allowed companies like Toy Biz to produce merchandise that dominated toy aisles worldwide.

10.10 Crossovers in Merchandising

Collaborative merchandise has allowed fans of both universes to celebrate their love for superheroes in unique ways:

- **DC's Crossover Lines**:
    - Team-ups with LEGO produced sets based on THE JUSTICE LEAGUE and THE DARK KNIGHT TRILOGY.

- **Marvel's Partnerships**:
    - Collaborated with brands like Adidas for exclusive Avengers-themed sneakers, bridging the gap between fandom and streetwear.

10.11 Seasonal and Event-Based Merchandising

Both universes capitalize on holidays and events to launch exclusive merchandise:

- **DC's Seasonal Releases**:
    - Batman-themed Halloween costumes and Superman Christmas ornaments became staples during their respective seasons.

- **Marvel's Event Tie-Ins**:
    - Released special merchandise during AVENGERS: ENDGAME that included limited-edition toys and clothing.

10.12 The Role of Fan Feedback in Product Development

Merchandise development increasingly incorporates fan input to create products that resonate:

- **DC's Response to Fan Demand**:
    - Fans clamored for more diverse collectibles, leading to products like DC BOMBSHELLS, featuring pin-up-style renditions of female heroes.

- **Marvel's Fan-Centric Lines**:
    - Lines like MARVEL LEGENDS were expanded based on fan polls to include obscure characters such as Beta Ray Bill.

10.13 The Impact of Merchandise on Pop Culture

Merchandise isn't just a revenue stream; it shapes public perceptions of superheroes:

- **DC's Influence**:
    - Items like Superman pajamas and Wonder Woman tiaras reinforce these characters as symbols of hope and empowerment for children.
- **Marvel's Reach**:
    - Characters like Spider-Man became global icons thanks to their ubiquity in toys and apparel, creating lifelong fans.

10.14 Licensing Controversies and Challenges

Licensing isn't without its pitfalls:

- **DC's Licensing Issues**:
    - Inconsistent branding between different eras led to confusion in merchandise design (e.g., retro Batman vs. modern Batman).

- **Marvel's Rights Complications**:
    - The division of character rights (e.g., X-Men with Fox, Spider-Man with Sony) created inconsistencies in how these characters were marketed.

10.15 Future Trends in Superhero Merchandise

The future of licensing and merchandise lies in innovation and digital integration:

- **Sustainable Products**:
    - Eco-friendly merchandise lines, such as biodegradable action figures and recyclable packaging, are on the rise.

- **Smart Merchandise**:
    - AR-enhanced toys and clothing that interact with apps, such as augmented reality Iron Man suits, are gaining popularity.

- **Personalized Products**:
    - Platforms that allow fans to customize items, such as creating action figures based on their likeness, are the next frontier.

Chapter 11: The Rise of Streaming and Digital Media

11.1 The Shift from Print to Digital

As digital technology advanced, both DC and Marvel adapted their publishing models:

- **DC's Digital Comics**: DC Universe Infinite app allowed fans to access a vast library of comics, reviving interest in classic storylines.

- **Marvel Unlimited**: Marvel's subscription model embraced binge-reading culture, with exclusive online content expanding their digital footprint.

11.2 Streaming as the New Battleground

The rise of platforms like Disney+ and HBO Max transformed how audiences consume superhero narratives.

- **DC's Strategy**:
    - DC Universe (later folded into HBO Max) created exclusive shows like TITANS, DOOM PATROL, and YOUNG JUSTICE: OUTSIDERS.
    - HBO Max elevated cinematic-style series such as PEACEMAKER and the upcoming LANTERNS.

- **Marvel's Domination on Disney+**:

    o WANDAVISION, LOKI, and THE FALCON AND THE WINTER SOLDIER became critical and commercial successes, tying directly into the MCU films.

    o Marvel's emphasis on interconnected storytelling expanded its universe further.

11.3 Challenges and Innovations in Streaming

- **Challenges**:

    o DC's fragmented platform strategy initially diluted its content visibility.

    o Marvel faced concerns about oversaturation and maintaining quality across numerous shows.

- **Innovations**:

    o Interactive storytelling, such as DC's experimental BATMAN: DEATH IN THE FAMILY animated film, where viewers could choose the story's path.

    o Marvel embraced docuseries like MARVEL STUDIOS: ASSEMBLED, offering fans behind-the-scenes content.

11.4 Competing in the Animated Arena

Both companies leveraged streaming to push animated content:

- **DC's Animated Series**: HARLEY QUINN, BATMAN: THE LONG HALLOWEEN, and JUSTICE LEAGUE DARK catered to mature audiences.

- **Marvel's Animated Efforts**: WHAT IF…? introduced multiverse concepts while celebrating the MCU's legacy.

11.5 Global Streaming and Localization

Streaming allowed both companies to tailor their content for international audiences:

- **DC's Reach**: Collaborated with global creators for animated features like BATMAN NINJA.

- **Marvel's Localization**: Characters like Shang-Chi were designed to resonate with Asian markets, blending cultural authenticity with superhero action.

11.6 The Future of Streaming Superheroes

- **DC's Future Plans**: Under James Gunn's leadership, HBO Max will integrate series and films more cohesively, starting with LANTERNS.

- **Marvel's Next Steps**: Disney+ will continue to expand its multiverse saga, using series to introduce major events like SECRET WARS.

- **Innovations to Expect**: Virtual reality experiences and interactive series may redefine fan engagement in the near future.

11.7 Regional Streaming Strategies and Partnerships

Both DC and Marvel have adapted their content for global audiences by forming regional partnerships and creating culturally specific content.

- **DC's Collaborations**:
    - Partnered with local animation studios for culturally infused content, such as BATMAN NINJA in Japan.
    - Released regionally exclusive series, like BATMAN: THE AUDIO ADVENTURES, which debuted on specific platforms.

- **Marvel's Regional Focus**:
    - Launched exclusive deals with Hotstar in India for quicker releases.
    - Characters like Kamala Khan (MS. MARVEL) were crafted to resonate with South Asian audiences, reflecting Marvel's increasing focus on representation.

11.8 Data Analytics and Audience Behavior

Streaming platforms leverage data analytics to shape the type of content produced:

- **DC's Data-Driven Decisions**:
    - Analyzing viewership trends on HBO Max to decide on spin-offs (e.g., THE PENGUIN following THE BATMAN).
    - Engaging fans with surveys to gauge interest in niche characters and stories.

- **Marvel's Fan Insights**:
    - Monitoring Disney+ viewership to greenlight projects like ECHO and IRONHEART.

- Using fan feedback from streaming forums to refine narrative arcs.

11.9 Expanding Digital Fan Engagement

Digital platforms are increasingly used to connect with fans directly:

- **Virtual Events**: DC's FANDOME provided fans with virtual panels, trailers, and exclusive sneak peeks, redefining fan interaction during the pandemic.

- **Interactive Media**: Marvel's integration of AR apps allowed fans to unlock special features, such as exclusive comic covers and behind-the-scenes videos.

11.10 Challenges of Multiversal Storytelling on Streaming Platforms

The complexities of multiverse narratives have posed unique challenges:

- **DC's Approach**:
    - Standalone series like STARGIRL maintained independence while subtly referencing larger universes.
    - Balancing multiple timelines (THE FLASH) without overwhelming casual viewers.

- **Marvel's Approach**:
    - Series like LOKI and WHAT IF...? introduced multiverse concepts, which sometimes required extensive context from prior films.

- o Criticism of over-reliance on interconnectedness, making it difficult for new viewers to jump in.

11.11 The Influence of Fan-Driven Platforms

Fan-created content on platforms like YouTube and Twitch has shaped how DC and Marvel approach their streaming strategies:

- **DC's Response**: Collaborating with influencers to promote shows and creating fan-centric events based on popular fan theories.

- **Marvel's Response**: Encouraging fan speculation through cryptic trailers and hidden Easter eggs in series like WANDAVISION.

Conclusion: A Legacy of Heroes

The Power of Stories

As we turn the final page of this exploration, one truth becomes undeniable: superheroes are more than entertainment—they are reflections of humanity's hopes, fears, and aspirations. Through their rivalry, DC and Marvel have created stories that transcend the boundaries of fiction, evolving into modern myths that resonate with people across generations and cultures.

From the bustling streets of New York to the shadowy alleys of Gotham, from the cosmic expanses of Asgard to the idyllic paradise of Themyscira, these two universes have built worlds that inspire and challenge us. They remind us that even in the face of darkness, light prevails; even when hope seems lost, heroes rise.

Unity in Diversity

Though DC and Marvel approach heroism differently—DC with its godlike, mythic figures, and Marvel with its relatable, flawed characters—they share a common goal: to inspire. Both universes teach us that heroism is not about perfection but about perseverance, sacrifice, and standing up for what's right.

Superman and Spider-Man, Wonder Woman and Captain Marvel, Batman and Iron Man—each embodies a unique perspective on courage and resilience. Together, they reflect the diversity of human experience, showing us that heroes come in all forms.

From Rivalry to Revolution

This rivalry has never been just about competition. It's been a crucible of creativity, where each challenge, each milestone, has propelled both DC and Marvel to greater heights. Their stories have inspired blockbuster films, immersive video games, innovative streaming series, and merchandise that turns symbols into cultural touchstones.

Through the decades, they've also mirrored societal changes, tackling issues of race, gender, equality, and identity. In doing so, they've reminded us that heroes are not only a product of their times but also a force for change.

The Future of Heroism

What lies ahead for DC and Marvel? Perhaps it's virtual reality adventures where fans can live as their favorite heroes. Maybe it's AI-driven, personalized narratives, where the story evolves based on the choices you make. Or perhaps it's entirely new forms of storytelling that we can't yet imagine.

What's certain is that superheroes will continue to evolve, finding new ways to inspire and connect us. As technology advances and new voices emerge, DC and Marvel's legacies will remain vibrant, reflecting the values and struggles of each generation.

A Final Word

The rivalry between DC and Marvel isn't about division—it's about the shared love for stories that inspire us to be better. Whether you see yourself in the godlike ideals of Superman or the human struggles of Spider-Man, these characters remind us that anyone can rise to the occasion and become a hero.

So, whether you're #TeamDC or #TeamMarvel, or even if you just love a good story, one thing is certain: the world is better with both.

Here's to the heroes who have shaped our past, the legends who define our present, and the ones who will inspire our future.

Because in the end, the story of DC and Marvel isn't just theirs—it's ours.

References

This book was created with the assistance of artificial intelligence tools, which contributed to the research, content organization, and development of ideas. The AI system synthesized general knowledge, public domain information, and creative analysis to produce the content.

No external books, articles, or direct sources were used in the creation of this book. Any historical references to DC Comics, Marvel Comics, or their associated characters and universes are based on widely recognized information available in the public domain.

Acknowledgment of AI Assistance

This book was developed with the help of artificial intelligence tools. While AI contributed to research, drafting, and analysis, all editorial decisions and final content oversight were conducted by the author.